SCIENCE LIBRARY
WILD ANIMALS

SCIENCE LIBRARY
WILD ANIMALS

Steve Parker

Consultants: Chris Pellant and Helen Pellant

First published in 2004 by Miles Kelly Publishing Ltd
Bardfield Centre Great Bardfield Essex CM7 4SL

2 4 6 8 10 9 7 5 3

Copyright © 2004 Miles Kelly Publishing Ltd
All rights reserved. No part of this publication may be reproduced, stored in
a retrieval system, or transmitted by any means, electronic, photocopying,
recording or otherwise, without the prior permission of the copyright holder.

British Library Cataloguing-in-Publication Data
A catalogue record for this book is available from the British Library

ISBN 1-84236-285-2

Printed in China

Editorial Director Anne Marshall

Editor Jenni Rainford

Editorial Assistant Teri Mort

Design Concept Debbie Meekcoms

Design Stonecastle Graphics

Copy Editor Rosalind Beckman

Consultants Chris Pellant and Helen Pellant

Proofreader Hayley Kerr

Indexer Hilary Bird

www.mileskelly.net
info@mileskelly.net

Third-party website addresses are provided by Miles Kelly Publishing
in good faith and for information only, and are suitable and accurate at the time of going to press.
Miles Kelly Publishing Ltd disclaims any responsibility for the material contained therein.

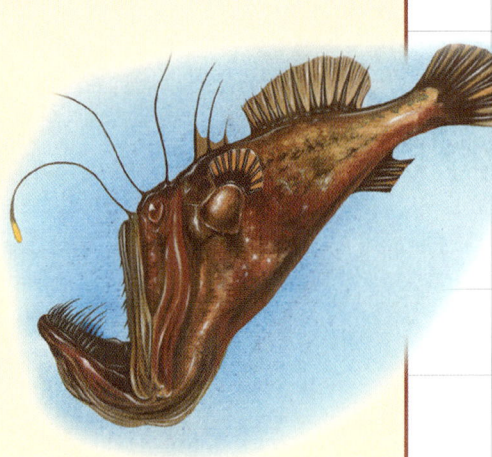

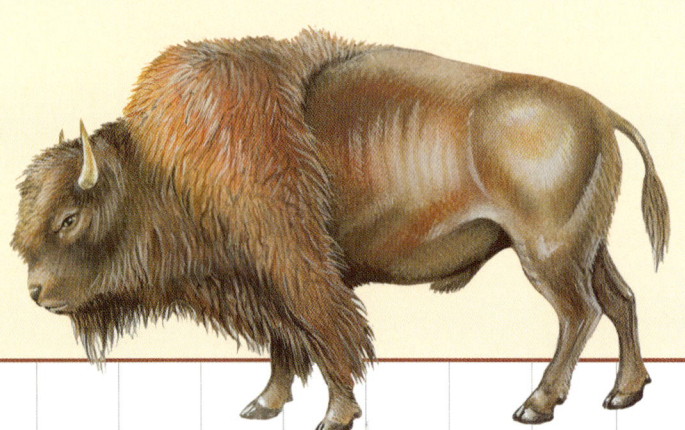

Contents

All kinds of animals 8–9

Mammals 1 10–11

Mammals 2 12–13

Mammals 3 14–15

Birds 1 16–17

Birds 2 18–19

Reptiles 20–21

Amphibians 22–23

Fish 24–25

Insects 1 26–27

Insects 2 28–29

More than eight legs 30–31

Shells and pincers 32–33

From molluscs to worms 34–35

Glossary 36–37

Index 38–40

How to use this book

WILD ANIMALS is packed with information, colour photos, diagrams, illustrations and features to help you learn more about science. Do you know how an aardvark digs for food or how big the wingspan of an albatross is? Did you know that female tarantulas wrap their eggs in silk or that the goliath beetle weighs more than 100 grams? Enter the fascinating world of science and learn about why things happen, where things come from and how things work. Find out how to use this book and start your journey of scientific discovery.

It's a fact
Key statistics and extra facts on each subject provide additional information.

Main text
Each page begins with an introduction to the different subject areas.

Main artwork
Each topic is clearly illustrated. Some illustrations are labelled, providing further information.

Record facts
Discover the superlatives within this box.

Birds 1

BIRDS ARE the only creatures with feathers. These protect the bird and form a large, light wing surface for flying. Feathers also help regulate a bird's body heat – like mammals, birds are warm-blooded. Some birds have feathers for camouflage (blending into the surroundings), while others have brightly coloured feathers to warn off predators or attract a mate. All birds have a beak, which is made of a strong, horn-like substance. The beak is shaped to eat certain foods. All birds also have scaly legs with clawed toes, and breed by laying eggs, usually in a nest made by the parents.

◀ Most parent birds, such as the golden eagle, care for their chicks (babies) and bring them food. These larger birds look after their chicks for longer. A young eagle does not leave its nest for about ten weeks.

The heaviest flying bird is the kori bustard, which can weigh up to 20 kg

IT'S A FACT
- There are about 9000 species of birds – this is twice as many species as mammals.
- There are 18 species in the penguin group, and 65 in the pelican group – including darters, cormorants, tropic birds, gannets and boobies.
- The owl group contains 205 species.

Birds of prey
Some of the largest and fiercest birds are raptors, or birds of prey. There are more than 300 species including eagles, condors, vultures, hawks, buzzards, kites, falcons, harriers and kestrels. They have powerful toes with sharp claws called talons to seize prey and a pointed, hooked beak to tear lumps of flesh. Most have big eyes and hunt by sight.

Read further > seizing prey
pg11 (e22)

BIRDS
Widest wingspan
- Wandering albatross
- Marabou stork
- Andean condor
- Swan

Check it out!
- http://www.enchanted...subjects/birds/Allabo...
- http://www.idahopt...birdsofprey/bird.htm

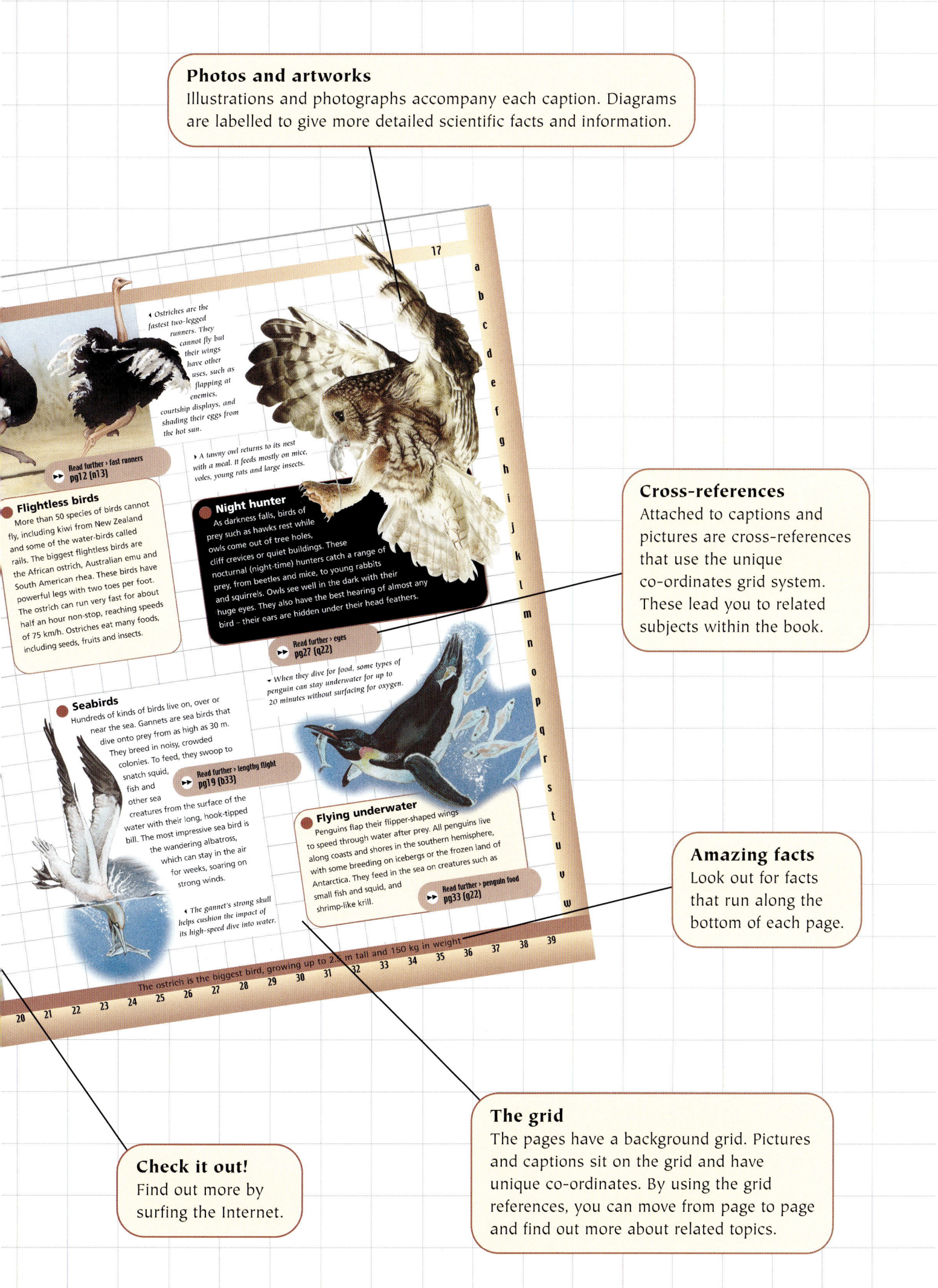

Photos and artworks
Illustrations and photographs accompany each caption. Diagrams are labelled to give more detailed scientific facts and information.

◀ Ostriches are the fastest two-legged runners. They cannot fly but their wings have other uses, such as flapping at enemies, courtship displays, and shading their eggs from the hot sun.

▶ Read further > fast runners
pg12 (n13)

Flightless birds
More than 50 species of birds cannot fly, including kiwi from New Zealand and some of the water-birds called rails. The biggest flightless birds are the African ostrich, Australian emu and South American rhea. These birds have powerful legs with two toes per foot. The ostrich can run very fast for about half an hour non-stop, reaching speeds of 75 km/h. Ostriches eat many foods, including seeds, fruits and insects.

▶ A tawny owl returns to its nest with a meal. It feeds mostly on mice, voles, young rats and large insects.

Night hunter
As darkness falls, birds of prey such as hawks rest while owls come out of tree holes, cliff crevices or quiet buildings. These nocturnal (night-time) hunters catch a range of prey, from beetles and mice, to young rabbits and squirrels. Owls see well in the dark with their huge eyes. They also have the best hearing of almost any bird – their ears are hidden under their head feathers.

▶ Read further > eyes
pg27 (q22)

Cross-references
Attached to captions and pictures are cross-references that use the unique co-ordinates grid system. These lead you to related subjects within the book.

▼ When they dive for food, some types of penguin can stay underwater for up to 20 minutes without surfacing for oxygen.

Seabirds
Hundreds of kinds of birds live on, over or near the sea. Gannets are sea birds that dive onto prey from as high as 30 m. They breed in noisy, crowded colonies. To feed, they swoop to snatch squid, fish and other sea creatures from the surface of the water with their long, hook-tipped bill. The most impressive sea bird is the wandering albatross, which can stay in the air for weeks, soaring on strong winds.

▶ Read further > lengthy flight
pg19 (b33)

Flying underwater
Penguins flap their flipper-shaped wings to speed through water after prey. All penguins live along coasts and shores in the southern hemisphere, with some breeding on icebergs or the frozen land of Antarctica. They feed in the sea on creatures such as small fish and squid, and shrimp-like krill.

▶ Read further > penguin food
pg33 (q22)

◀ The gannet's strong skull helps cushion the impact of its high-speed dive into water.

The ostrich is the biggest bird, growing up to 2.5 m tall and 150 kg in weight

Amazing facts
Look out for facts that run along the bottom of each page.

Check it out!
Find out more by surfing the Internet.

The grid
The pages have a background grid. Pictures and captions sit on the grid and have unique co-ordinates. By using the grid references, you can move from page to page and find out more about related topics.

All kinds of animals

THE WORLD is full of animals. They live on top of the highest mountains, at the bottom of the deepest seas, in tropical rainforests and in the cold, icy wastes of the polar regions. Some animals are so weird and so different from those we keep at home or see on farms or at the zoo that we might wonder whether they are animals at all. The study of animals is vitally important – to save wildlife and conserve the wonder and beauty of the natural world for the future, and to improve our farming and food supplies for an increasing world population.

Read further > adapting
pg11 (d22)

What is an animal?

Animals come in many different shapes and sizes, and live in a wide variety of habitats. So what defining features do they share that make them all animals? Like plants, their bodies are made of many microscopic parts called cells. However, unlike most plants, they take food into their bodies by eating it and breaking it down, rather than by building it up from simple minerals. They sense or detect features of their surroundings such as light or sound. Most animals can move about at some stage in their lives.

▼ Different parts of the world have their own distinctive types of animal, which adapt, survive and reproduce in various habitats.

IT'S A FACT

- The biggest animals are 1 million million times larger than the smallest ones.
- More than 999 out of every 1000 kinds of animals that ever lived, such as dinosaurs, died out long ago.
- The total number of kinds, or species, of animals is probably more than 10 million.

The first animals lived in oceans over 1000 million years ago

Wild Animals

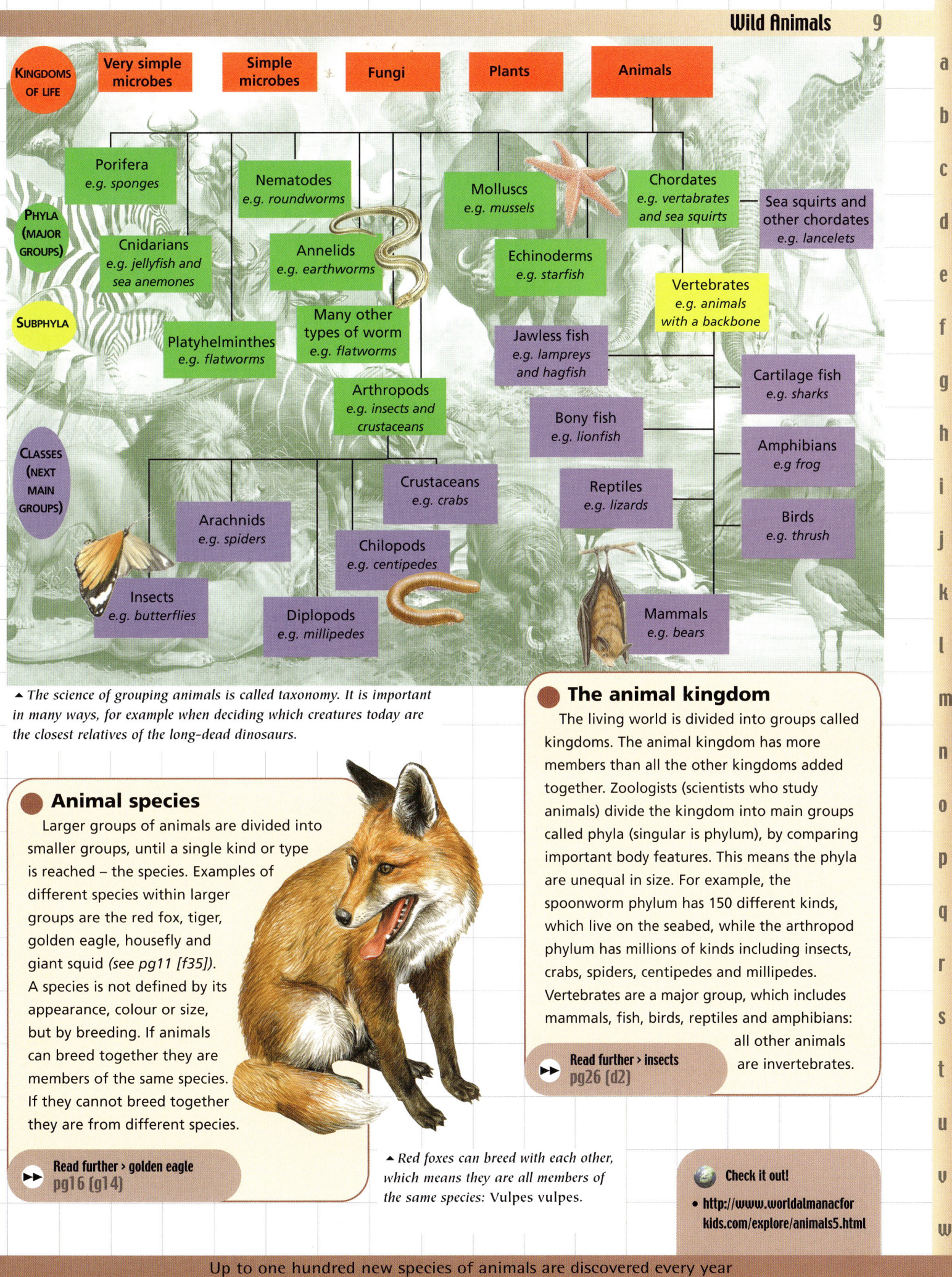

▲ The science of grouping animals is called taxonomy. It is important in many ways, for example when deciding which creatures today are the closest relatives of the long-dead dinosaurs.

● The animal kingdom

The living world is divided into groups called kingdoms. The animal kingdom has more members than all the other kingdoms added together. Zoologists (scientists who study animals) divide the kingdom into main groups called phyla (singular is phylum), by comparing important body features. This means the phyla are unequal in size. For example, the spoonworm phylum has 150 different kinds, which live on the seabed, while the arthropod phylum has millions of kinds including insects, crabs, spiders, centipedes and millipedes. Vertebrates are a major group, which includes mammals, fish, birds, reptiles and amphibians: all other animals are invertebrates.

Read further › insects
pg26 (d2)

● Animal species

Larger groups of animals are divided into smaller groups, until a single kind or type is reached – the species. Examples of different species within larger groups are the red fox, tiger, golden eagle, housefly and giant squid *(see pg11 [f35])*. A species is not defined by its appearance, colour or size, but by breeding. If animals can breed together they are members of the same species. If they cannot breed together they are from different species.

Read further › golden eagle
pg16 (g14)

▲ Red foxes can breed with each other, which means they are all members of the same species: *Vulpes vulpes*.

Check it out!
• http://www.worldalmanacfor kids.com/explore/animals5.html

Up to one hundred new species of animals are discovered every year

Mammals 1

MAMMALS ARE the most familiar class of animals, because human beings are members. Typical mammals have a body covering of fur or hair, are warm-blooded (their body temperature stays at the same high level despite changes in the surroundings) and feed their babies on milk made by the mother in body parts called mammary glands. However, there are exceptions. The biggest mammals of all, such as whales in the sea and elephants on land, have almost no hair or fur. And some mammals go into a long winter sleep called hibernation, when their body temperatures fall to just above freezing.

IT'S A FACT

- Throughout the world there are about 4500 different species of mammals.
- The mammal with the largest numbers around the world – more than 6000 million – is the human.
- The most common truly wild mammal is the crabeater seal – they number about 15 million.
- The 34 species of seals, sea-lions and walruses belong to the mammal group pinnipeds, which means 'flipper-feet'.

Bears

The eight kinds of bears are members of the small mammal family, ursidae. Their foods differ greatly. Most bears eat large amounts of plant foods, such as leaves, fruits, berries and nuts, as well as meat. The giant panda eats almost nothing but bamboo. Yet the diet of the polar bear of the far north consists almost entirely of meat. It rivals the brown or grizzly bear as the biggest land predator, weighing over half a tonne and standing 3 m tall.

Read further > biggest predator
pg11 (e22)

▶ Polar bears are almost pure white, while their close cousins, the American black bears, are mostly black.

Insect eaters

The insectivores (insect eaters) are mostly smallish mammals such as moles, shrews and hedgehogs. They have small, sharp teeth and eat insects, grubs, slugs, worms and similar juicy creatures. There are about 365 species, including the rat-like tenrecs from Africa, and the rare, long-nosed solenodons that live on some Caribbean islands.

▲ There are 12 species of hedgehogs and most have sharp spines like this European hedgehog – but the desert hedgehog has coarse fur.

Read further > insects / worms
pg26 (d2); pg35 (b33)

Check it out!

- http://www.yahooligans.com/content/animals/mammals
- http://www.iwrc-online.org/kids/Facts/Mammals/bats.htm

A sperm whale can hold its breath for two hours

Wild Animals   11

Read further > molluscs
pg34 (n2)

▲ The world's biggest predator, the 50-tonne sperm whale, attacks the largest invertebrate animal, the giant squid.

● Life in the water

Cetaceans are porpoises, whales and dolphins that live in tropical seas and rivers. They are hairless mammals whose bodies have adapted fully to life in the water. Their front limbs are flippers, their back limbs are missing and their tails have wide flaps on either side, called flukes, for swimming. There are about 83 species of cetaceans and they are all carnivorous – they eat other animals. These great whales consume vast amounts of krill – tiny, shrimp-like creatures, while sperm whales prey on large fish and seals.

● Meat-eating mammals

Any animal that eats mainly meat is known as a carnivore. Confusingly, there is also a group of mammals officially called the Carnivora. It includes dogs, foxes, jackals, bears, raccoons, weasels and stoats, civets and linsangs, hyaenas and cats.

Read further > sharp teeth
pg25 (b22)

▲ Hyaenas have keen senses to track their victims, fierce claws and long, sharp teeth – canines – to stab and rip prey.

● Bats

Bats are the second-largest mammal group, with almost 1000 species. Most bats are small, live in tropical rainforests and fly at night to catch gnats, moths and similar flying insects. The flying foxes or fruit bats, with about 175 species, are bigger and eat plant foods such as fruits, seeds and sap. A bat's front limbs are actually wings that have a thin, stretchy membrane or layer, attached to very long finger bones.

Read further > flying insects
pg26 (h16)

▶ Fruit bats rest with their wings wrapped around their bodies.

ANIMAL FACTS

• The biggest mammal, and the biggest animal of all, is the blue whale. It is 30 m in length and weighs more than 100 tonnes.

• The smallest mammals are shrews on the ground and bats in the air. The pygmy shrew has a head and body smaller than the human thumb. The hog-nosed bat's wings are each about as long as a human finger.

• The longest-lived mammals include the rare, seldom-seen beaked whales – some may be more than 150 years old.

The largest bats have wings measuring 1.6 m across

Mammals 2

IT'S A FACT
- There are more than 1650 species of rodents: this is the largest group of mammals.
- The rabbit and hare group, lagomorphs, has 80 species.
- The ungulates or hoofed mammals number about 245 species.

MOST MAMMALS are herbivores – plant eaters. The largest plant-eating group, rodents, make up 40 per cent of the mammal group. They include rats, mice, squirrels, beavers, porcupines and guinea pigs, and their cousins from South America, known as cavies. Rabbits and hares look like rodents because of their long front teeth but they belong to a different mammal order known as lagomorphs. Another large plant-eating order is the ungulates or hoofed mammals. These are divided into two types: the odd-toed ungulates – with one or three toes – such as horses, zebras, asses, tapirs and rhinos, and the even-toed ungulates – with two or four toes – such as pigs, peccaries, hippos, camels, deer, giraffes, antelopes, gazelles, cattle, sheep and goats.

Rodents
Rodents live all over the world, in almost every land habitat. One species, the beaver, can swim underwater for almost 1 km, holding its breath and keeping its nostrils and ears shut. The rodent's special feature is its front teeth, called incisors. These are very long with straight, sharp edges like chisels. They keep growing through life, so rodents can gnaw hard foods like nuts and roots, without wearing away their teeth.

▶▶ Read further > underwater
pg15 (m31); pg17 (s31)

▲ Beavers gnaw through tree trunks in minutes with their long, ever-growing incisor teeth.

▶ Most ungulates, like zebra, are fast runners. They are able to outrun most predators from a young age.

Odd-toed ungulates
Horses, zebras, rhinos and tapirs are called odd-toed ungulates because they have an odd number of toes per foot, each capped with a hard hoof. Horses and zebras have just one toe per foot and their legs are long and slim for running in open habitats such as grasslands. They are grazing animals, and feed mainly on grass that they chew with their powerful jaws and cheek teeth.

▶▶ Read further > ungulates
pg13 (b22)

The tallest mammal is the giraffe, measuring more than 5 m from its head to the tip of its toes

Wild Animals

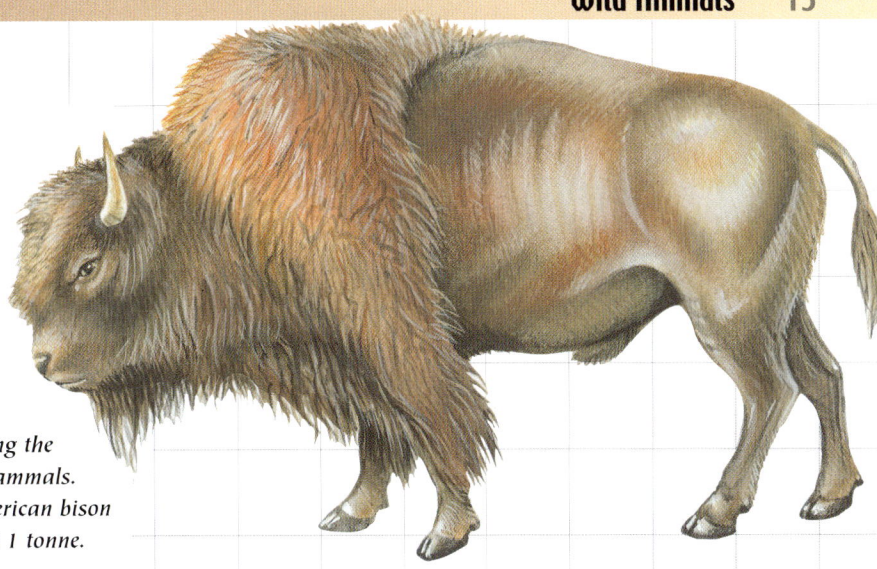

Even-toed ungulates

The bison is an even-toed ungulate or 'cloven hoofed' mammal. Herds on the North American prairies were almost wiped out by European settlers in the 1500s but have since recovered some of their numbers. European bison are slightly smaller and live in thick forests, mainly in Poland and Belarussia.

Read further › biggest mammal pg11 (r32)

▶ Bison are among the biggest hoofed mammals. A large male American bison can weigh almost 1 tonne.

◀ Dromedary (one-humped) camels have broad feet to keep them steady on desert sand and long eyelashes to protect them in sand storms.

Humps store fat

▶ Bactrian (two-humped) camels have thick fur that helps to keep out the cold of the Mongolian high grasslands.

Trunk and tusk

Elephants are the largest land mammals. A large, male African savannah elephant can stand 4 m tall and weigh more than 8 tonnes. All elephants are plant-eaters. They may look like hoofed mammals but they have their own order, called proboscidea.

▼ Elephant tusks are greatly enlarged upper incisor teeth and the trunks are a very long combination of upper lip and nose.

Read further › herbivores pg15 (e31)

Camel humps

Both species of camel – the one-humped dromedary of Africa, the Middle East and Australia, and the two-humped Bactrian of Central Asia – have been domesticated (bred by people) for milk, meat, hides and carrying. The camel group also includes the camel's South American relations – the guanaco and vicuna in the wild, and their domesticated descendants, the llama and alpaca.

ANIMAL FACTS

• The Sumatran rhinoceros, which has red coloured hair is a relative of the woolly rhinoceros of the last ice age.

• For many years it was believed there were only two types of elephant: African and Asian. But there are three.

• There are two species of African elephant: the African savannah elephant, large with curved tusks, prefers open country; the African forest elephant, slightly smaller with straighter tusks, likes thick woodland. Being different species, they cannot breed with each other.

Check it out!
- http://www.enchantedlearning.com/subjects/mammals/classification/Ungulates.shtml

The biggest rodent is the capybara of South America, weighing up to 60 kg

Mammals 3

SOME GROUPS of mammals have many members while others have very few. The marsupial group consists of about 290 species, including kangaroos and Virginia opossums, while the tubulidentata has only one living species – the aardvark from Africa. There are only four species of dugongs and manatees, also known as sirenians or 'sea cows'. These bulky plant eaters of shallow coastal waters have front limbs like paddles and flipper-shaped tails. Another group, the monotremes or egg-laying mammals, has just five species, including the duck-billed platypus and echidnas.

IT'S A FACT

- The primate group includes lemurs, monkeys, and humans, and numbers about 350 species.
- There are only two species of colugos, or flying lemurs, which live in Southeast Asian tropical forests and eat mainly plants.

▼ The Virginia opossum may have 18 babies in one litter. After growing in her pouch for 6-8 weeks, they ride clinging to her back.

Cows of the sea

Sirenians are the only sea mammals that eat mainly plants, although they may occasionally eat small fish for added nutrients. Their diet of seagrass, seaweeds and other aquatic vegetation is low in nourishment, so a sirenian may need to consume up to one-quarter of its body weight each day. Their closest mammal cousins are probably not seals or whales, but the elephants and hoofed mammals.

▶▶ Read further > hoofed mammals
pg13 (b22)

▲ Manatees weigh more than half a tonne. They have round, spoon-like tails to help them move through the water.

Marsupials

Marsupials live mainly in Australia, with some species found in South America and Southeast Asia. Only one kind, the Virginia opossum, has spread to North America. Many smaller marsupials resemble other types of mammals – there are marsupial mice and rats, shrews and cats, and even marsupial anteaters and moles.

▶▶ Read further > marsupials
pg13 (e31)

Check it out!

- http://www.enchantedlearning.com/subjects/mammals/classification/Ungulates.shtml

The biggest marsupial is the red kangaroo, weighing up to 90 kg

Powerful digger

The aardvark emerges at night and may travel more than 20 km in search of ant nests and termite mounds. It has a variety of common names, such as earth-pig, African anteater and ant-bear. Its closest mammal relations are probably the hoofed mammal group, ungulates. The aardvark's teeth are among the most unusual of any mammal: it has no front incisors or canines but cheek teeth or molars that grow continuously. In mammals, the number and types of teeth are important in working out which of the groups are most closely related.

▶▶ Read further › ungulates
pg12 (n13)

▲ The aardvark has a long, sensitive snout to sniff out food in the dark. The nostrils are surrounded by fine hairs that keep out dust as the aardvark digs into its prey's nest.

ANIMAL FACTS

• The primate mammals include the lesser apes – nine species of gibbons – all in Southeast Asia. They swing through trees, using their very long, powerful arms and hook-like hands. The largest gibbon, the siamang, is one of the loudest of any mammals, almost equalling the South American howler monkey – the noisiest of all land animals.

• The largest meat-eating marsupial, the Tasmanian devil, has a fierce and aggressive reputation, but it rarely gets into fights with others of its kind. It eats many small animals from insects to possums. Some people keep Tasmanian devils as tame, friendly pets.

▶ A baby kangaroo is called a joey. It is as small as a grape when it is born. After six months in the pouch it is ready to leave for short periods.

Bounding along

Marsupials are pouched mammals because in most types, the female has a pocket-like pouch of skin on her front. Her baby is born at a tiny, undeveloped stage and crawls into the pouch, where it feeds on her milk and grows over many weeks. Kangaroos and wallabies are large plant eaters native to Australia. They bound along on their two enormous back legs, using their thick tail for balance.

▶▶ Read further › Australian emu
pg17 (g22)

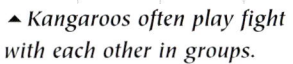

▲ Kangaroos often play fight with each other in groups.

Egg-laying mammals

One of the most extraordinary mammals is the platypus of Australia. It has a duck-like beak or bill, a flat tail and webbed feet like a beaver. It is one of the few mammals that does not give birth to babies, but lays eggs in a deep burrow. The eggs hatch after about ten days and the mother then feeds her babies on milk, as do other mammals. The four species of echidnas or 'spiny anteaters' of Australia and Southeast Asia are also egg-layers.

▶▶ Read further › beaver
pg12 (p2)

▶ The platypus feeds in streams and pools on small creatures. Its beak is very sensitive to touch and it can feed at night, just by feeling for food.

The biggest monkeys are drills and mandrills, at 40 kg

Birds 1

BIRDS ARE the only creatures with feathers. These protect the bird and form a large, light wing surface for flying. Feathers also help regulate a bird's body heat – like mammals, birds are warm-blooded. Some birds have feathers for camouflage (blending into the surroundings), while others have brightly coloured feathers to warn off predators or attract a mate. All birds have a beak, which is made of a strong, horn-like substance. The beak is shaped to eat certain foods. All birds also have scaly legs with clawed toes, and breed by laying eggs, usually in a nest made by the parents.

IT'S A FACT

- There are about 9000 species of birds – this is twice as many species as mammals.
- There are 18 species in the penguin group, and 65 in the pelican group – including darters, cormorants, tropic birds, gannets and boobies.
- The owl group contains 205 species.

Birds of prey

Some of the largest and fiercest birds are raptors, or birds of prey. There are more than 300 species including eagles, condors, vultures, hawks, buzzards, kites, falcons, harriers and kestrels. They have powerful toes with sharp claws called talons to seize prey, and a pointed, hooked beak to tear off lumps of flesh. Most have big eyes and hunt by sight.

▶▶ Read further > seizing prey
pg11 (e22)

◀ Most parent birds, such as the golden eagle, care for their chicks (babies) and bring them food. These larger birds look after their chicks for longer. A young eagle does not leave its nest for about ten weeks.

BIRDS

Widest wingspan	Width
Wandering albatross	3.6 m
Marabou stork	3.2 m
Andean condor	3 m
Swan	2.8 m

Check it out!

- http://www.enchantedlearning.com/subjects/birds/Allaboutbirds.html

The heaviest flying bird is the kori bustard, which can weigh up to 20 kg

◀ Ostriches are the fastest two-legged runners. They cannot fly but their wings have other uses, such as flapping at enemies, courtship displays, and shading their eggs from the hot sun.

▶▶ Read further > fast runners
pg12 (n13)

▶ A tawny owl returns to its nest with a meal. It feeds mostly on mice, voles, young rats and large insects.

● Flightless birds

More than 50 species of birds cannot fly, including kiwi from New Zealand and some of the water-birds called rails. The biggest flightless birds are the African ostrich, Australian emu and South American rhea. These birds have powerful legs with two toes per foot. The ostrich can run very fast for about half an hour non-stop, reaching speeds of 75 km/h. Ostriches eat many foods, including seeds, fruits and insects.

● Night hunter

As darkness falls, birds of prey such as hawks rest while owls come out of tree holes, cliff crevices or quiet buildings. These nocturnal (night-time) hunters catch a range of prey, from beetles and mice, to young rabbits and squirrels. Owls see well in the dark with their huge eyes. They also have the best hearing of almost any bird – their ears are hidden under their head feathers.

▶▶ Read further > eyes
pg27 (q22)

● Seabirds

Hundreds of kinds of birds live on, over or near the sea. Gannets are sea birds that dive onto prey from as high as 30 m. They breed in noisy, crowded colonies. To feed, they swoop to snatch squid, fish and other sea creatures from the surface of the water with their long, hook-tipped bill. The most impressive sea bird is the wandering albatross, which can stay in the air for weeks, soaring on strong winds.

▶▶ Read further > lengthy flight
pg19 (b33)

▼ When they dive for food, some types of penguin can stay underwater for up to 20 minutes without surfacing for oxygen.

● Flying underwater

Penguins flap their flipper-shaped wings to speed through water after prey. All penguins live along coasts and shores in the southern hemisphere, with some breeding on icebergs or the frozen land of Antarctica. They feed in the sea on creatures such as small fish and squid, and shrimp-like krill.

▶▶ Read further > penguin food
pg33 (g22)

◀ The gannet's strong skull helps cushion the impact of its high-speed dive into water.

The ostrich is the biggest bird, growing up to 2.5 m tall and 150 kg in weight

Birds 2

A BIRD'S BEAK or bill is used for feeding, preening the feathers (keeping them clean and combed), holding materials for building a nest and pecking at enemies. The shape of the beak reveals the type of food the bird eats. The toucan has a huge and colourful but very lightweight beak, which can reach fruits and berries at the tips of branches. The parrot's massive, curved beak works like a nutcracker to split the hardest seeds. Many hummingbirds have long, needle-like beaks to probe into flowers and sip the sweet, energy-rich nectar. Common birds such as crows and blackbirds have all-purpose beaks for eating plants and small animals such as worms.

IT'S A FACT

- More than half of all bird species, some 5400, belong to the group called passerines or perching birds.
- The next largest group is the swifts and hummingbirds, with 425 species.
- There are 380 species of woodpeckers and toucans.

▼ The sword-billed hummingbird has an extremely long beak and a long tongue for extracting nectar from flowers.

Spearing fish

There are nearly 200 species of kingfishers all around the world. Most have beaks that are long and sharp, like a dagger, for spearing fish. The Eurasian kingfisher has brightly coloured feathers of blue, green and orange, and nests in a tunnel in the riverbank. However, the largest type of kingfisher – the kookaburra of Australia – rarely eats fish, preferring to eat small mammals and lizards, and lives in woods, parks and gardens. Its raucous cackle earns it the nickname 'laughing jackass'.

◀ The Eurasian kingfisher watches for prey from a perch overlooking a river.

Read further > lizards
pg21 (r31)

Beaks

A bird's beak or bill is its feeding tool, so it is important to keep the beak clean and undamaged. A bird often jabs its beak into loose soil to remove sticky material and debris. Under the beak's covering of keratin are the bones of the upper and lower jaws – the maxilla and mandible. These move or flex with the head, to prevent the beak being damaged. In general, the shorter the beak, the more force it can produce for eating harder foods.

◀ The sickle-billed vanga uses its beak to probe bark to find insects.

▶ The upper and lower portions of the crossbill's beak cross over so it can prise open pine cones.

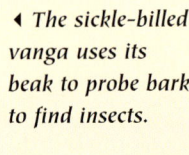

ANIMAL FACTS

- The outer, horny covering of a bird's beak is made of keratin (just like human nails).
- Most birds have three types of feathers: large, flattened flight feathers on the wings, smaller contour feathers to cover and protect the body, and fluffy down feathers to maintain warmth.

Check it out!

- http://www.iwrc-online.org/kids/Facts/Birds/birds.htm
- http://www.inhs.uiuc.edu/chf/pub/virtualbird/student/les1.html
- http://www.tpwd.state.tx.us/adv/birding/beginbird/kidbird.htm

In Africa, red-billed queleas destroy more farm crops than locusts do

Wild Animals

Nests

Some birds do not make nests. The guillemot lays its egg on the ledge of a seaside cliff, while some plovers lay their speckled eggs among the same-coloured pebbles of a shingle beach. But most birds dig or construct a nest from whatever materials are handy, to protect their eggs. The stork makes one of the biggest nests from sticks and twigs on the roof or chimney of a house.

▲ Swifts spend winter in Africa before travelling (migrating) to Europe and East Asia for summer to breed. In the evening they fly low in groups and gradually gain height to sleep in the air.

On the wing

The Eurasian swift spends so much time in the air that its legs and feet are tiny and weak. It twists and turns as it hunts flies and other insects. Its beak is small but gapes wide, with a fringe of whiskery bristles to funnel food into the mouth. Swifts can also mate, swoop down to drink, and fly very high to sleep – all on the wing. If a swift lands on a flat surface it can hardly stand and finds it difficult to take off.

Read further > insects pg27 (b35)

▲ The female song thrush sits on (incubates) her eggs in a nest made from grass and moss, usually made in the fork of a tree.

Read further > laying eggs pg21 (m22)

Calls and songs

Most birds make sounds using a specialized voice box called a syrinx in the neck. Calls are usually short and harsh to warn of danger. Songs are longer and more tuneful. Each bird has an in-built ability to sing and mimic other birds.

Read further > warning pg16 (d2)

◀ Mockingbirds of North and South America are so called because they imitate the calls of other bird species.

Breeding together

Some birds such as gulls, seabirds and the tall waders, flamingos, breed in vast groups or colonies. Each pair of flamingos makes a nest shaped like a raised bowl in the mud of a shallow lake. Both parents feed the chick for about two weeks. Then all the chicks gather together in a vast crowd or 'creche'. Some flamingo colonies number half a million adults and chicks.

Read further > seabirds pg17 (n24)

▼ Flamingos feed, breed, wade and fly in flocks. They feed on tiny creatures in water.

A large bird such as a swan has 25,000 feathers

Reptiles

MOST OF the 8000 or so species of reptile have scaly skin, lay eggs and are 'cold-blooded'. This means, unlike mammals and birds, they cannot make heat inside their bodies. So most reptiles inhabit warm areas, basking in the sun. In scrublands and deserts reptiles sleep through long droughts. Reptiles live in all habitats except at the coldest poles – and turtles and sea-snakes are found in oceans. The major reptile groups are crocodilians, turtles and tortoises, snakes and lizards, and amphisbaenids – tropical worm-like creatures that live mostly underground.

IT'S A FACT

- One of the world's most poisonous snakes is the bushmaster, from tropical America, which grows to 3.5 m in length.
- The largest lizard, the komodo dragon, is more than 3 m in length.
- The only lizards with poison bites are the gila monster and Mexican beaded lizard, both of southern North America.

Deadly predators

There are 23 kinds of crocodilians – crocodiles, alligators, caimans and one species of gharial. Crocodilians are powerful hunters, they lurk in swamps, lakes and rivers waiting for prey. Crocodiles are found in Asia, Africa and Australia, while alligators and caimans are usually found in North, Central and South America. They make good hunters because they can approach prey through water stealthily, with only their eyes and nostrils above the surface as they move.

▼ *The alligator's snout is broad for seizing large prey.*

Read further > eggs
pg23 (j22)

▼ *The gharial has a long, thin snout and slim jaws for catching fish.*

ANIMAL FACTS

- One of the rarest and strangest reptiles is the tuatara. It lives on a few islands off New Zealand and emerges from its burrow at night to eat mainly insects. Its eggs take more than one year to hatch, and some tuataras live for more than 75 years.
- There are five species of caiman – a type of alligator. They live in Central and South America.

▲ *Crocodile snouts are designed to kill large prey. The alligator's snout is broad for seizing large prey.*

▼ *The black caiman's snout tapers at the end to catch small prey.*

Check it out!

- http://www.all-creatures.org/aip/nl-23nov2001-reptiles.html
- http://www.oneworldmagazine.org/tales/crocs/index.html

The largest reptile is the saltwater crocodile, 7 m long and 1 tonne in weight

Wild Animals 21

● Smooth but not slippery

Snakes range from the 1-m python snake and the 200-kg anaconda, which constrict or squeeze their prey to death, to tiny thread-snakes smaller than a pencil. All hunt living prey but fewer than 50 types are deadly poisonous to humans. These include adders, vipers, mambas and cobras. The king cobra is the longest poisonous snake: it is 5 m in length. Its main prey is other snakes.

▲ The puff adder, found in Africa, is highly venomous and is responsible for the most snake attacks on humans.

Read further › laying eggs pg19 (b22)

◀ A cobra's jaws are so loose and bendy, it can swallow prey that is bigger than its own head, such as a small rodent.

● Slow but safe

Tortoises are chelonians that live on land. Most eat plants but a few also consume small animals. Some survive in the driest deserts, where they burrow into the soil to escape heat and drought. The desert tortoise lays its eggs in a hole or under a rock or log: when these hatch some weeks later, the babies must fend for themselves.

Read further › eggs pg15 (m31)

▲ The desert tortoise has especially large front legs, wide feet and stout claws, to burrow into the dry soil to avoid the hottest part of the day.

● Ocean wanderers

About 290 kinds of turtles and tortoises make up the reptile group called chelonians. Their main feature is the shell, made of a domed upper part, the carapace, and a flatter underside, the plastron. The carapace and plastron are formed from up to 60 curved bony plates, covered by another layer of horny plates. Some have hard, bony shells to protect against land predators; others have a streamlined carapace for swimming easily through water.

Read further › hard body casing pg32 (d2)

▼ Female sea turtles come ashore only to lay eggs in a hole on the beach. Males never touch dry land after hatching.

▶ The frilled lizard of Australia is up to 70 cm in length and its frill can be extended to a width of 25 cm.

● Variety of lizards

Lizards are the most wide-ranging and varied reptiles. The Galapagos iguana dives under the water to eat seaweed, the Nile monitor lizard is powerful enough to catch small antelopes, and the chameleon flicks out a sticky-tipped tongue as long as its body to grab flies. Most lizards have a long tail and four legs, but some lizards, such as slow-worms and skinks, have no limbs.

Read further › worms pg35 (b22)

Giant tortoises can live to 150 years of age

Amphibians

THE NAME 'amphibian' means 'both lives', because most amphibians live on land and breed in water. Many of the 5000 species live in water when young and breathe using gills like fish. As they grow older most amphibians spend more time on land, lose their gills and breathe with their lungs. In a change in shape known as metamorphosis, amphibians develop from eggs, to larva or tadpole, to fully grown adults. The three main groups of amphibians are frogs and toads, newts and salamanders, and the smallest group, called caecilians, which are worm-like creatures.

IT'S A FACT
- The flying frog has huge feet with webbed toes that it spreads like parachutes to glide.
- The female Suriname toad carries her eggs in pouches of skin on her back.
- The biggest frog or toad is the goliath frog of West Africa. It is almost as large as a soccer ball.

Frogs and toads
Many frogs and toads have skin that makes a horrible-tasting or poisonous fluid, so predators, such as snakes and spiders, usually avoid them. Many predators build up a resistance to the milder toxins, so the frog's skin has evolved to produce a stronger poison. Toads are usually larger than frogs, have lumpier skin, and waddle rather than leap.

◄ *The colours of poison-dart frogs warn predators of their poisonous skin.*

▶▶ **Read further > defence**
pg25 (m33)

Salamanders
Giant salamanders are the largest of all the amphibians. Some species are exceptional in size: the Japanese giant salamander can grow to 1.4 m; the Chinese giant salamander can grow up to 1.5 m. Like newts, salamanders retain their tails into adulthood. Salamanders have a powerful bite and feed on shellfish, freshwater fish, worms and insects.

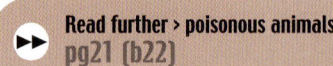
▶▶ **Read further > poisonous animals**
pg21 (b22)

ANIMAL FACTS
- A type of salamander, the rare axolotl, lives in a few lakes in Mexico. It keeps its larval shape and gills all through its life. However, its reproductive organs develop, so it can breed even though it looks immature.
- Amphibians are cold-blooded and in cold regions they survive long winters in a state of inactivity known as torpor. The spring peeper frog of North America can be frozen solid for weeks, then it thaws out without harm because it has a natural 'anti-freeze' substance in its blood and other body fluids.

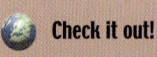
Check it out!
- http://www.yahooligans.com/content/animals/amphibians
- http://www.fonz.org/animals/af-amphibians.htm

▲ *The hellbender of North America grows to 80 cm in length.*

Australia's water-holding frog can survive buried in the desert for up to five years

Wild Animals

Newts

Newts are a type of salamander that tend to stay in water for long periods, even when air-breathing adults. Like salamanders, newts do not need to feed often as they do not use a lot of energy. However, like all amphibians, when newts do feed they flick out their long tongues to grab prey, such as worms, slugs, snails, grubs, flies and other insects and small fish.

▸ The Eastern newt is red, orange or brown with black spots. It lives on land for up to four years of its early life. After this it returns to the water to develop into an adult.

Read further > insects pg27 (b24)

Worm-like amphibians

Caecilians, also known as gymnophiones, live mostly in the damp tropics among soil and leaves on the forest floor or in pools and swamps. They have no legs, very small eyes, and resemble large earthworms, growing up to 60 cm in length. Like other amphibians they are predators and feed on soil creatures, including earthworms.

▲ Caecilians burrow powerfully, pushing soil with their broad snouts.

Read further > earthworms pg35 (b22)

Life cycle

The life cycle of the common frog begins when the female lays a clump of jelly-covered eggs (called spawn) in fresh water. The eggs are then fertilized by the male's sperm. The eggs hatch into larvae or tadpoles. Tadpoles have gills and a long tail but no legs, and eat water plants. Gradually they metamorphose into adults. Their legs grow, their tails shrink and their lungs develop to breathe air.

Read further > eggs hatching pg21 (b33)

Frog spawn (eggs) float on top of water

Tadpoles hatch from eggs

Tadpoles grow legs and change into froglets

Froglet loses tail and grows into adult frog

Adult toad

Adult newt

◂ The common frog's life cycle is similar to those of toads and newts. Frogs lay eggs in a clump. Toads lay eggs in long strings or 'necklaces'. Newts lay eggs singly.

The gastric-brooding frog has tadpoles that develop in its stomach

Fish

A TYPICAL FISH lives in water, has a long, slim body, large eyes, a finned tail that swishes from side to side for swimming, body fins to control its movements, a covering of scales, and feather-like gills on either side of the head that take in oxygen from the water. However, many fish lack one or more of these features. Eels are long and thin like snakes and usually scaleless, lungfish can breathe out of water, and many catfish have leathery skin or bony plates rather than scales.

ANIMAL FACTS

- The biggest hunting fish is the great white shark or white pointer. The biggest grow to about 9 m in length and weigh up to 3 tonnes.

- At 12–14 m in length and weighing more than 10 tonnes, the whale shark is the biggest fish. But it is not a fierce hunter like the great white shark. It filters small plants and animals (plankton) from seawater, using comb-like rakers on the insides of its gills.

Read further > predators
pg16 (g14); pg20 (o2)

IT'S A FACT

- The smallest fish, the dwarf goby, is as long as the word 'fish' and lives in streams and pools on the Philippine Islands.

- One of the longest fish is the eel-shaped oarfish of open oceans that grows to more than 8 m – one is caught about every ten years.

▼ The 6-m tiger shark prefers warm-blooded victims such as monk seals. However, it will eat almost anything, from sea turtles to rotting, leftover food thrown from ships.

Ocean killers

There are about 330 species of sharks. As well as eating plankton, which includes plant matter, all sharks eat meat, either catching victims or scavenging from dead animals. Unlike most fish, a shark's skeleton is made of cartilage (gristle) rather than bone.
A shark also has unusual scales called denticles that are tiny and tooth-shaped. Much larger denticles form the shark's teeth, which are always being worn away or broken off to be replaced by new ones.

Check it out!
- http://www.iwrc-online.org/kids/Facts/Fish/fish.htm
- http://www.kidzone.ws/sharks
- http://www.fishid.com/facts.htm

The biggest freshwater fish is the Amazonian arapaima, weighing 200 kg and measuring 4.5 m

Wild Animals 25

● Fish food

Different types of fish eat a huge variety of food. Piranhas have razor-sharp teeth and gather around a large animal in the water to tear off chunks of flesh. In fresh water, the pike lurks in weeds and dashes out to grab a victim in its huge mouth. Carp sift through mud for worms and other creatures. On coral reefs, butterfly fish and parrot fish eat tiny plants and animals growing on the rocks.

▼ *Piranhas live in South American rivers and swamps. They feed on other fish, insects, even fruit, but as a ferocious predatory group they can attack and kill small mammals and even humans.*

▶▶ Read further › teeth
pg12 (p2)

● 'Dino'-fish

Coelacanths lived during the age of dinosaurs, about 250 million years ago, and were thought to be extinct. However, in the 1930s a coelacanth was discovered in the Indian Ocean off southern Africa. Another type was found in the 1990s in the Celebes Sea off Southeast Asia. Fish like these may have developed their fins into legs to become the first amphibian, more than 350 million years ago.

▼ *Coelacanths have fleshy, muscular bases to their fins that they use to 'walk' over rocks.*

◀ *The stonefish is the world's most poisonous fish. It produces a deadly venom from dorsal spines along its side.*

● Bottom of the sea

Below about 500 m the sea is completely dark, so that colourful bodies are of no use. Most deep-sea fish, such as the gulper eel, viperfish and deep-sea anglerfish, are black. Some have tiny eyes and some no eyes at all. Others have huge eyes to detect what little light there is.

▶▶ Read further › colour
pg29 (i32)

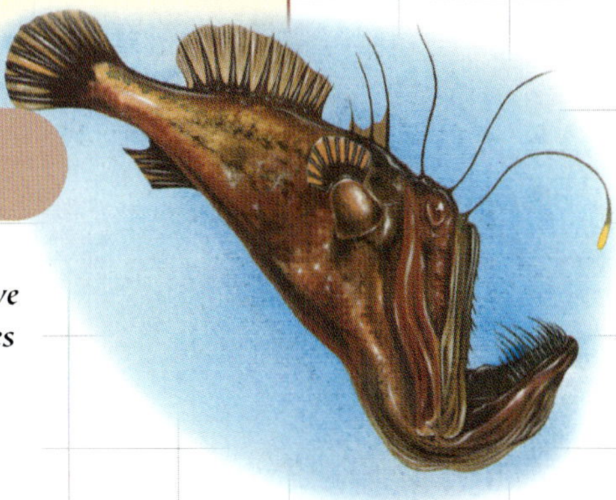

▼ *Deep-sea lanternfish make their own light with rows of glowing spots.*

▶ *Deep-sea anglerfish have a blob of flesh that dangles in front of them. This attracts smaller fish that think it might be edible.*

● Defence

Some fish defend themselves with poisons, which they can jab into enemies using their stiff, sharp fin spines. The lionfish or dragonfish of Southeast Asia has large, lacy-looking fins and bright colours to warn predators of its venom. In contrast, the stonefish is camouflaged as a piece of rock for protection.

◀ *The lionfish's organs are luminous (light reflects through).*

▶▶ Read further › poison
pg27 (b35); pg31 (e33)

The electric eel's shock is more than 600 volts – enough to kill a human

Insects 1

ARTHROPODS ARE invertebrate animals (lacking a backbone) with a hard outer body casing, and limbs with joints, rather than flexible tentacles. Insects are the biggest group of arthropods and the most numerous animals on Earth. More than 1 million species have been discovered. A typical adult insect has three body parts: head, thorax and abdomen. The head has the antennae or feelers, large eyes and mouthparts; the thorax bears the wings (usually four) and six legs; the abdomen contains the digestive and reproductive parts. Insects live in every land and freshwater habitat, from frozen polar regions and icy mountaintops to scrub, deserts, rivers and deep lakes. However, no insects dwell in the sea.

ANIMAL FACTS

• Most insects have short lives of a few months, but some survive for many years. The periodic cicada is a type of bug. It dwells as a young form or nymph in the soil, eating roots and other bits of plants, for up to 17 years.

• Cicadas are also the noisiest insects, and for their size, they make the loudest sounds of any animals. Only the males 'sing'. They vibrate thin, flexible patches of body casing, like drum skins, on either side of the abdomen.

IT'S A FACT

• Some cave crickets and cockroaches have antennae (feelers) that are ten times as long as their bodies, since they cannot see in total darkness underground and so must feel their way.

• About three in every ten species of insect are beetles.

Fast and fierce

Dragonflies are among the biggest, fastest and fiercest insects. They catch smaller insects, such as gnats, in mid-air, using their dangling legs like a scoop or basket, and then take the victim back to a favourite perch to eat. Each dragonfly has its own area or territory, which usually includes water, such as a pond or stream. It 'buzzes' rival dragonflies who come too near to chase them off their territory.

◂ Dragonflies have four wings and hunt using their huge eyes, which are larger than any other insect.

Read further › legs
pg17 (g22)

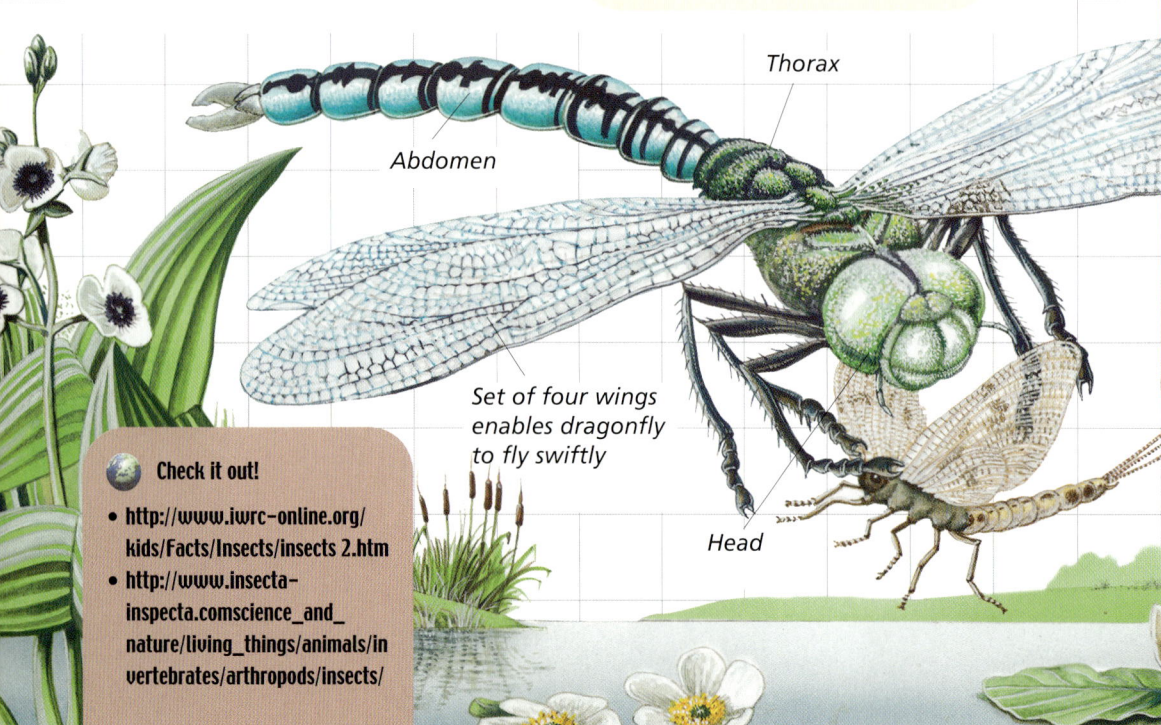

Thorax

Abdomen

Set of four wings enables dragonfly to fly swiftly

Head

Check it out!
• http://www.iwrc-online.org/kids/Facts/Insects/insects 2.htm
• http://www.insecta-inspecta.comscience_and_nature/living_things/animals/invertebrates/arthropods/insects/

The longest insects are tropical stick insects – they can reach 30 cm in length

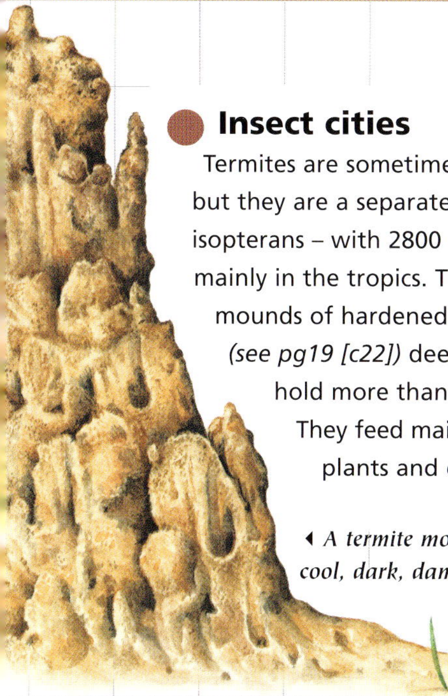

Wild Animals 27

● Insect cities

Termites are sometimes called 'white ants' but they are a separate group of insects – isopterans – with 2800 species that live mainly in the tropics. They build huge mounds of hardened mud, with a nest (see pg19 [c22]) deep inside that may hold more than 5 million termites. They feed mainly on bits of wood, plants and decaying matter.

◀ A termite mound keeps its occupants cool, dark, damp and protected.

Read further > nest building
pg19 (b22)

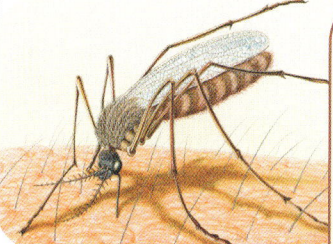

▲ The female mosquito, about 2 cm in length, feeds on animal and human blood.

● Insect pests

Mosquitos, a type of fly, have needle-like mouthparts to pierce human skin and suck blood. This causes an itchy spot on the skin and sometimes spreads serious diseases such as malaria, which can be fatal. Fleas have huge rear legs for jumping, no wings and suck blood in the same way as mosquitos. Many flies, cockroaches and similar insects feed in dirt and decay and spread germs carried on their bodies, legs and mouthparts.

Read further > sucking
pg29 (b22)

▼ The female praying mantis devours (eats) the male directly after they have mated.

▼ Great green bush crickets are also known as katydids. Most species mimic (take the appearance of) leaves or bark.

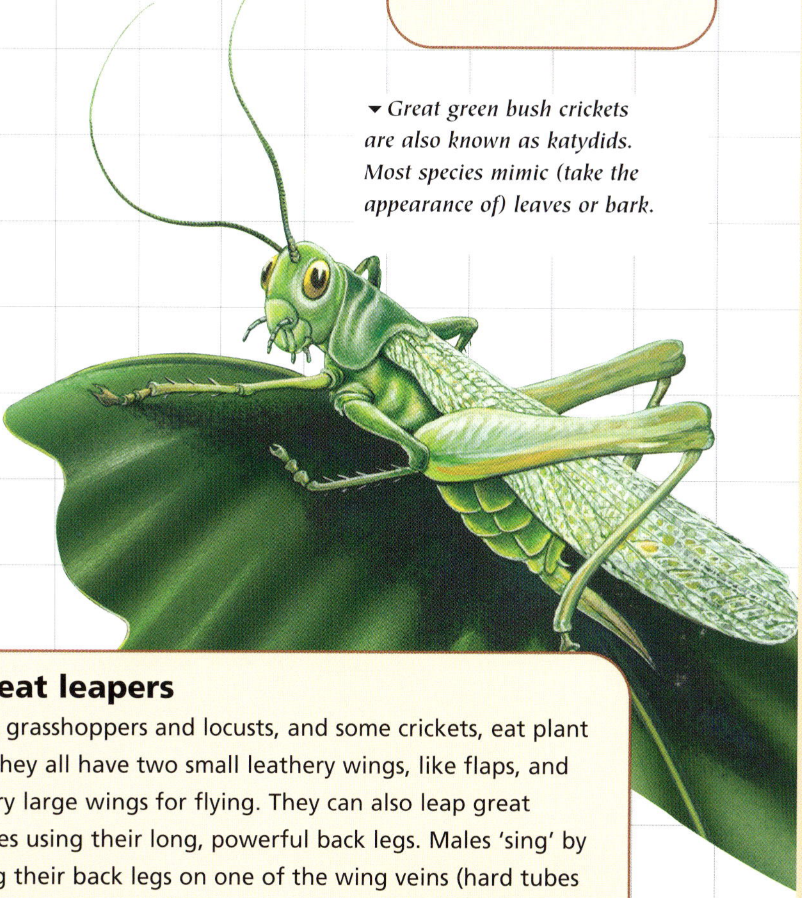

● Insect eyes

Read further > senses
pg11 (h32)

Almost all of the 2000 kinds of mantises (mantids) are fierce hunters. They grab prey with their front legs, which fold at the end like spiky scissors. An insect's eye is made of many separate parts, ommatidia, each detecting a tiny part of the scene. Mantids have huge eyes – each with more than 20,000 ommatidia. Mantids' wings are folded along their backs, ready to flash colour at their enemies.

● Great leapers

Most grasshoppers and locusts, and some crickets, eat plant food. They all have two small leathery wings, like flaps, and two very large wings for flying. They can also leap great distances using their long, powerful back legs. Males 'sing' by rubbing their back legs on one of the wing veins (hard tubes that support the wings), which has a row of 'teeth' like a tiny comb.

Read further > teeth / fangs
pg31 (e33)

The smallest insects are fairy-flies (types of wasps) – the size of this dot 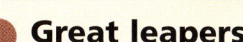.

Insects 2

> **IT'S A FACT**
> • The bulkiest insect is the goliath beetle, which is 20 cm long and weighs more than 100 g.
>
> • A caterpillar can increase its weight by more than 100 times in two weeks, which is one of the fastest growth rates of any animal.

NEARLY ALL insects hatch from eggs laid by the female. Only a few insect mothers, such as the earwig, care for their eggs or young. With some insects, such as grasshoppers and dragonflies, the young – nymphs – resemble their parents, although they are smaller and without wings. Nymphs gradually develop into adults by moulting (shedding their body cases) regularly. As their bodies go through little change, this type of development is incomplete metamorphosis. Other insects, such as butterflies, moths, beetles, bees, wasps and ants, have greater changes in body shape and experience a complete metamorphosis.

Complete metamorphosis

A butterfly's eggs hatch into small, wriggly young called larvae or caterpillars. The young eat huge amounts of food and shed their skins several times as they grow. They develop a hard body case and become inactive pupae, or chrysalises. After a time the pupa's casing splits and the adult insect emerges. Most caterpillars eat mainly leaves, while butterflies sip nectar from flowers.

Female butterfly lays tiny eggs, usually under leaves

Caterpillar hatches from eggs and eats leaves

Caterpillar becomes pupa

Adult butterfly emerges

Pupa's case splits open

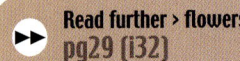
Read further > flowers
pg29 (i32)

ANIMAL FACTS

• Many species of beetles have larvae (grubs) called 'worms', because they are long, legless and wriggly. They include mealworms and woodworms.

• Glow-worms are adult beetles that shine in the dark to attract a mate.

• Many types of insect live in water when young, such as the nymphs of dragonflies, damselflies, caddisflies and mayflies.

▲ *Adult stonefly nymphs rarely fly. Instead they crawl among stream-bed rocks and pebbles.*

Incomplete metamorphosis

Stonefly nymphs live in fast-flowing streams. They have wide, low bodies and strong legs with sharp claws to cling to smooth rocks in the rushing water. They grow for two or three years, then emerge and shed their skins to become adult stoneflies. Adult stoneflies look like small, short-bodied dragonflies. They fly, eat and live for only a week or two, in order to breed.

Ants are, for their size, the strongest of all animals

Wild Animals

Hard wings

A beetle has four wings, but the front two, known as elytra, are strong and stiff. They normally lie over the beetle's back and cover and protect the larger, delicate flying wings that are folded beneath. Water beetles hunt tadpoles, worms and young fish in ponds and streams. They must rise to the surface regularly to refresh their air supplies that are in the form of tiny air bubbles stored under their elytra.

▼ Water beetles can fly away to another pond if the one they are in dries out.

Read further > tadpoles pg23 (j22)

Pollination

Bees play a vital role in the reproduction of plants. As they visit colourful flowers to collect sweet nectar and tiny pollen grains for food, some pollen from the flower brushes on to the bee's feet and rubs off when it lands on the next flower. This process is called pollination and is how pollen grains are transferred from flower to flower so that flowers can develop seeds. Many other insects, such as flies and beetles, pollinate flowers in the same way.

▼ A honeybee can make more than 500 visits to flowers in one day. The female honeybee carries pollen in a basket-shaped pouch on the hindlegs.

Read further > pollen pg17 (s31)

Bugs

More than 80,000 species of insects are known as bugs. Most bugs have four wings and long, thin mouthparts that are like needles to pierce victims and suck liquid food. Pondskaters skim over water to catch and drown their prey. Aphids (greenflies and blackflies), cicadas and treehoppers suck plant sap; bedbugs feed on human blood; and shieldbugs have a shield-like body covering, which is often brightly coloured.

Read further > blood sucking pg27 (b35)

▼ The pondskater glides across water, ready to squeeze its prey, which are usually animals trapped at the surface in its front legs before sucking out the juices.

Check it out!
- http://www.enchantedlearning.com/subjects/butterflies/toc.shtml
- http://www.uky.edu/Agriculture/Entomology/ythfacts/bugfun/trivia.htm

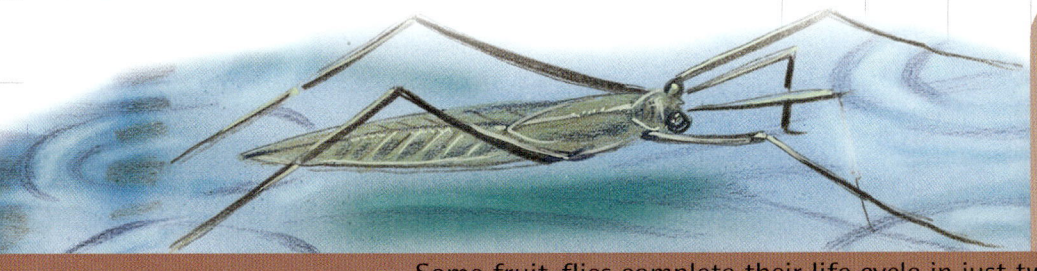

Some fruit-flies complete their life cycle in just two weeks

More than eight legs

ARTHROPODS include insects, millipedes (four legs on each body part or segment), centipedes (two legs per segment) and another huge group – the arachnids, which have two main body segments and eight legs. Arachnids include spiders and scorpions, which live on land, and their tiny cousins, mites and ticks, known as false-scorpions, which live in water.

IT'S A FACT

- There are more than 60,000 kinds of arachnids, living in all land habitats and a few freshwater ones, but not in the sea.
- The centipede group, chilopoda, numbers some 3000 species.
- There are more than 10,000 kinds of millipedes, diplopoda.

Centipedes and millipedes

'Centipede' means '100 feet' but most centipedes have up to 60 legs. They live mainly in tropical rainforests and are fast-moving night-time predators, using their fang-shaped, first pair of legs to jab and poison prey. The biggest species grow to 30 cm in length and their bite can cause extreme pain to humans. Some millipedes have only 24 feet, while others have more than 700 – but none can run fast. They are protected by their hard body casings and by a horrible-tasting or poisonous fluid that oozes from holes along the body.

▸ *Most millipedes feed at night on rotting leaves and old bits of plants.*

▶▶ Read further > biting
pg27 (b35)

▼ *Ticks are about 1 cm in length but they grow larger when they have eaten. Mites usually grow no larger than 1 mm in length.*

Mites and ticks

Mites are tiny, eight-legged cousins of spiders. Most are smaller than this 'o' and live in the soil. A handful of earth from a forest might contain more than 1000 of them. Other types live as parasites on larger animals, sucking their blood or munching their skin, fur or feathers. Ticks are also blood-sucking parasites that live on many animals, from sheep to cats, and even occasionally on people.

▶▶ Read further > blood-sucking
pg27 (b35)

BIGGEST SPIDERS

Spider	Width
South American bird-eating spider	28 cm
Central American running spider	25 cm
African hercules spider	20 cm
Cardinal spider	14 cm

A garden spider takes an hour to spin its web

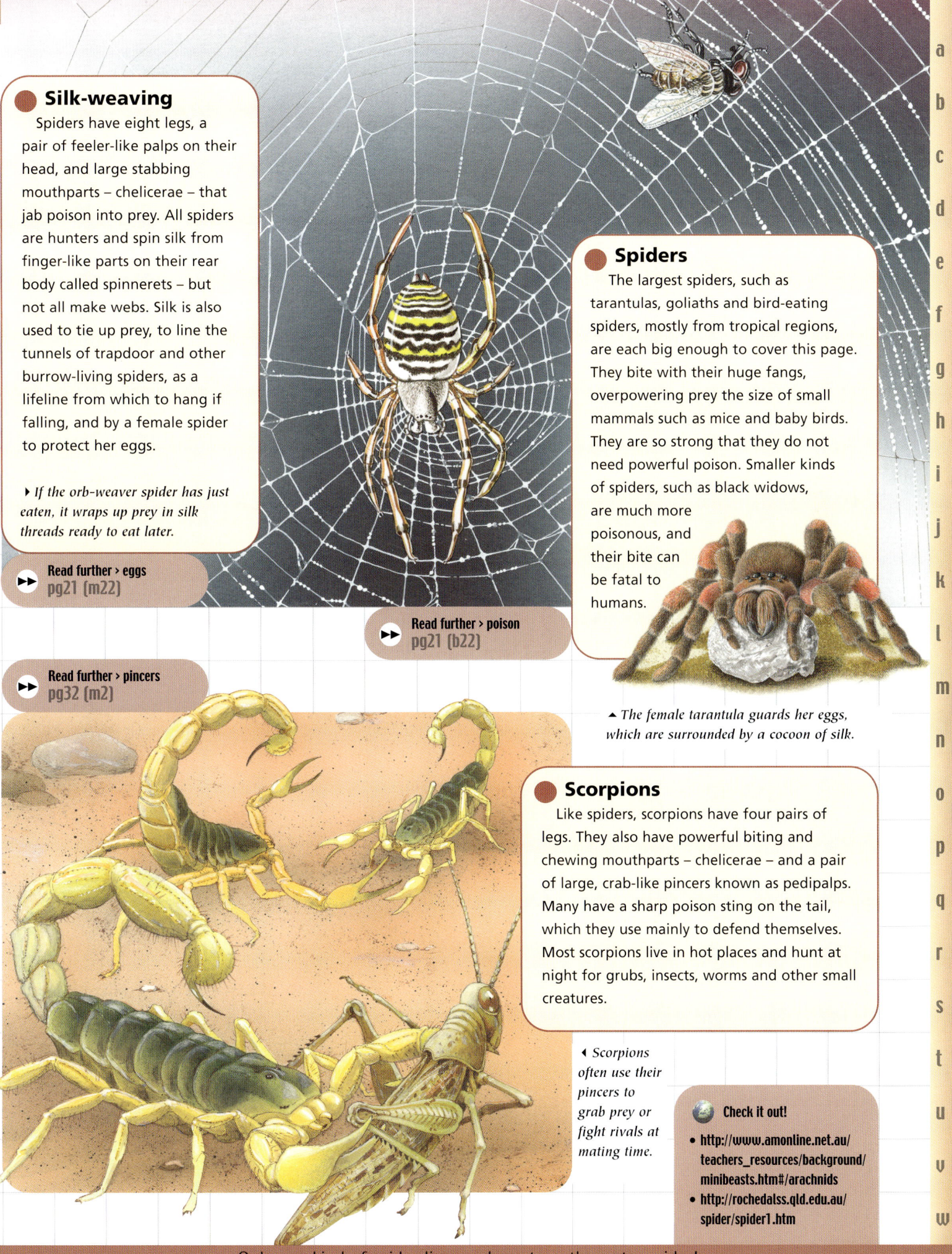

Silk-weaving

Spiders have eight legs, a pair of feeler-like palps on their head, and large stabbing mouthparts – chelicerae – that jab poison into prey. All spiders are hunters and spin silk from finger-like parts on their rear body called spinnerets – but not all make webs. Silk is also used to tie up prey, to line the tunnels of trapdoor and other burrow-living spiders, as a lifeline from which to hang if falling, and by a female spider to protect her eggs.

▶ If the orb-weaver spider has just eaten, it wraps up prey in silk threads ready to eat later.

▶▶ Read further > eggs
pg21 (m22)

▶▶ Read further > pincers
pg32 (m2)

Spiders

The largest spiders, such as tarantulas, goliaths and bird-eating spiders, mostly from tropical regions, are each big enough to cover this page. They bite with their huge fangs, overpowering prey the size of small mammals such as mice and baby birds. They are so strong that they do not need powerful poison. Smaller kinds of spiders, such as black widows, are much more poisonous, and their bite can be fatal to humans.

▶▶ Read further > poison
pg21 (b22)

▲ The female tarantula guards her eggs, which are surrounded by a cocoon of silk.

Scorpions

Like spiders, scorpions have four pairs of legs. They also have powerful biting and chewing mouthparts – chelicerae – and a pair of large, crab-like pincers known as pedipalps. Many have a sharp poison sting on the tail, which they use mainly to defend themselves. Most scorpions live in hot places and hunt at night for grubs, insects, worms and other small creatures.

◀ Scorpions often use their pincers to grab prey or fight rivals at mating time.

Check it out!
- http://www.amonline.net.au/teachers_resources/background/minibeasts.htm#/arachnids
- http://rochedalss.qld.edu.au/spider/spider1.htm

Only one kind of spider lives underwater – the water spider!

Shells and pincers

CRUSTACEANS OR 'crusty-cases' are animals such as crabs, lobsters, prawns, shrimps, krill and barnacles, with a hard outer body casing and several pairs of jointed legs. There are more than 40,000 species, and most live in the sea. They are the equivalent of insects on land – they swarm in the oceans in their billions, and are important food for larger sea creatures such as penguins, seals, dolphins and whales. A few crustaceans such as water-fleas and crayfish live in fresh water. Even fewer survive on land, and these include sand-hoppers on beaches and woodlice (sowbugs) under rotting bark.

ANIMAL FACTS

- Goose-barnacles are crustaceans with a bendy stalk that attaches to a piece of driftwood, a pale shell-like body case, and limbs that poke out to gather food.
- Lobsters are dark green or blue in colour when they are alive – they only turn red when they are cooked.
- The giant Japanese spider crab can grow to measure 3 m across between the tips of its outstretched pincers.

Legs and claws

An old lobster may still be growing after 50 years. This tough creature belongs to the decapod or 'ten-legs' crustacean group. Eight legs are for walking, and the other two limbs are large pincers for feeding and defence. They breathe underwater through gills along the side of their bodies, under the casing.

Shrimps

All crustaceans hatch from eggs and drift in the sea as young larvae. They make up much of the plankton that is eaten by bigger sea creatures. Shrimps go through several larval stages with different body shapes before turning into adults. Tadpole shrimps often hatch after heavy storms if the eggs have survived the dry weather.

▲ The mantis shrimp uses its claws to smash crab shells to crack them open.

Read further > larvae pg28 (r2)

▶ Spiny lobsters gather at seabed areas in spring before 'marching' in lines of migration, clinging to each others' tails to deeper water, to breed.

Read further > eight legs pg30 (b22)

A big lobster may be 1 m in length and weigh more than 50 kg

Wild Animals

◂ Most copepods are almost too small to see and are eaten by baby fish and other small sea creatures.

▸ In water, porcelain crabs often become tangled in the tentacles of sea anemones.

● Copepods

Copepods are crustaceans that are among the most numerous of all animals. Each one has a shield-like body case and fringed limbs that it waves to swim. It also uses these to gather food. In the sea, copepods feed and reproduce in the brightly lit water close to the surface. Vast clusters or swarms of copepods feed on microscopic plants and animals. Along with krill, copepods are the the main food for fish and other sea animals.

▸▸ Read further > sea animals
pg15 (m31)

● Feeding

Most crabs are scavengers, feeding on any edible scraps and remains. On some tropical shores there are thousands of porcelain crabs. They feed by scooping up clumps of mud with their claws, and filtering out tiny particles of food with the bristle-like hairs on their mouthparts. On the sea shore, the porcelain crab hides under rocks, waiting for prey.

▸▸ Read further > mouthparts
pg31 (o32)

● Smaller crustaceans

The water flea or pond flea, daphnia, is a crustacean named after its similarity to an insect. It has two antennea (feelers), which has many branches like tiny trees. They are a very common inhabitant of ponds and streams. Because ponds often dry out, water fleas have developed drought-resistant eggs. If it lays the eggs and the pond dries out, the eggs do not hatch until the water returns. Another small crustacean, fish lice, are blood-sucking parasites just like real lice (though real lice are insects, not crustaceans). These flat-bodied, tough-cased crustaceans have powerful suckers on their underside. They stick to fish and draw out their body fluids.

▸ The water flea waves its antennae like oars to row through the water. Inside the rear of its body are large eggs, ready to be laid.

▸▸ Read further > insects
pg26 (d2)

IT'S A FACT

- The largest crustacean is the giant spider crab of the north-west Pacific Ocean, with a body the width of a soccer ball and spindly pincers 1.5 m in length.
- Some swarms of krill are more than 100 km long and contain 10 trillion individuals.
- Brine-shrimps can hatch from eggs that have been wetted after being dried out and preserved for more than 1000 years.

Check it out!
- http://www.allaboutnature.com/subjects/Crab.shtml
- http://www.enchantedlearning.com/subjects/invertebrates/crustacean/index.shtml

The robber crab can stay out of water for days – and climb trees!

From molluscs to worms

CREATURES WITH hard shells such as snails, oysters, mussels and whelks belong to the huge animal group known as molluscs. However, some molluscs, including slugs and squid, have no outer shell at all. An unusual group of animals is the echinoderms, which includes starfish and sea urchins. They usually have a body shape that is radial, like a wheel with spokes, rather than two-sided with left and right, like other animals. There are also thousands of other types of strange-looking animals such as jellyfish and sponges.

● ANIMAL FACTS

• One of the longest but thinnest animals is the ribbon-worm or bootlace-worm (nemertean). This amazing animal lives on the seashore, feeds on tiny animals, and may grow to more than 30 m – longer than a blue whale!

• Roundworms (nematodes) are seldom seen, but they live almost everywhere, including soil, water and inside plants and animals. There are more than 20,000 kinds of roundworms, and some grow to 9 m in length inside great whales.

▼ Rock pools support a huge variety of life including crustaceans such as crabs and lobsters, molluscs such as snails and mussels, and sea anemones.

● Molluscs

Molluscs range from tiny slugs as small as 2 mm, to giant squid with a body and tentacles 20 m in length. Most have a hard shell either outside or inside the body. Molluscs include many seashore 'shellfish' such as clams, limpets and cowries. Octopus and squid grab victims with their suckered tentacles and bite off pieces with the mouth at their centre, which is shaped like a parrot's beak.

▲ Squid are fast swimmers, often reaching speeds of 50 km/h.

▶▶ Read further > hard shells
pg21 (m22)

Sea anemones (cnidarian)

● Echinoderms

All echinoderms live in the sea. Their name means 'spiny-skinned', and most sea urchins and a few starfish have sharp spines, sometimes poisonous. Other types of echinoderm include sea cucumbers, which are usually sausage-shaped and sort through seabed mud for food particles. Sea lilies are also echinoderms.

Starfish (echinoderm)

▶▶ Read further > sharp spines
pg10 (i15)

The bite of a blue-ringed octopus can kill a human in 20 minutes

Wild Animals

All kinds of worms

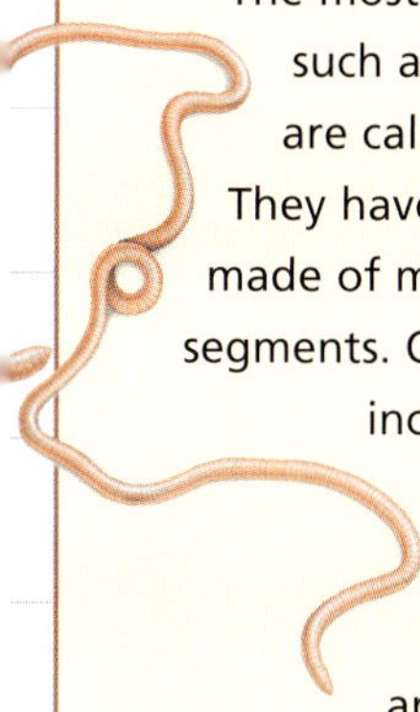

The most familiar worms, such as earthworms, are called annelids. They have a long body made of many sections or segments. Other annelids include ragworms, fanworms and tubeworms on the seashore and in the sea, and leaf-shaped leeches that suck blood from other animals.

▶▶ **Read further > blood-sucking**
pg27 (b35)

IT'S A FACT

- There are more than 100,000 different species of molluscs.
- The echinoderm phylum numbers over 6000 species.
- Annelids, such as earthworms, consist of 12,000 species.

Jellyfish

Jellyfish, sea anemones and coral polyps are all members of the cnidarian group, containing almost 10,000 different species. Most live in the sea and have a jelly-like body or stalk and a ring of tentacles that sting their prey. Coral polyps build cup-shaped cases of hard minerals around themselves; most corals gradually build up over time to form the unusual shapes of coral reefs.

▶▶ **Read further > stinging prey**
pg31 (o32)

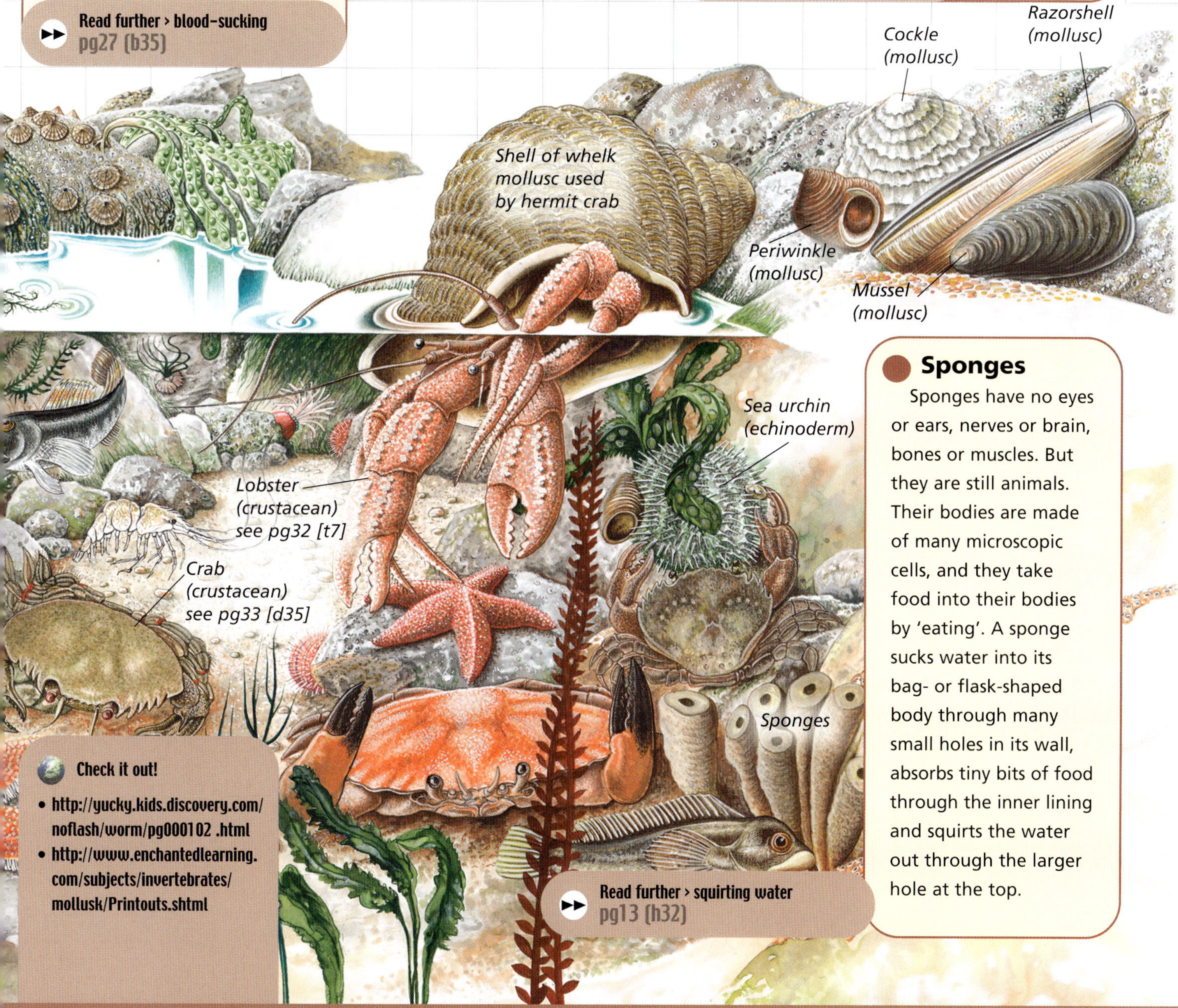

Shell of whelk mollusc used by hermit crab

Cockle (mollusc)

Razorshell (mollusc)

Periwinkle (mollusc)

Mussel (mollusc)

Lobster (crustacean) see pg32 [t7]

Crab (crustacean) see pg33 [d35]

Sea urchin (echinoderm)

Sponges

Sponges

Sponges have no eyes or ears, nerves or brain, bones or muscles. But they are still animals. Their bodies are made of many microscopic cells, and they take food into their bodies by 'eating'. A sponge sucks water into its bag- or flask-shaped body through many small holes in its wall, absorbs tiny bits of food through the inner lining and squirts the water out through the larger hole at the top.

Check it out!
- http://yucky.kids.discovery.com/noflash/worm/pg000102.html
- http://www.enchantedlearning.com/subjects/invertebrates/mollusk/Printouts.shtml

▶▶ **Read further > squirting water**
pg13 (h32)

The sting of a coneshell – a type of mollusc – can kill a human in 20 minutes

Glossary

Abdomen The lower main body in many kinds of animals. It usually contains the digestive, excretory and reproductive parts.

Antennae Long, slim parts on the head of animals, such as insects, often called 'feelers' that sense touch, movement and taste.

Arthropod Any invertebrate animal.

Camouflage When an animal is shaped, coloured and patterned to merge or blend in with its surroundings.

Carnivore An animal that eats mainly meat.

Cell The smallest part of life. Some living things are just single cells. Animal bodies consist of millions of different cells.

Chelicerae Fang-shaped or pincer-like biting parts on the head of animals, such as spiders and scorpions.

Class The groups into which a phylum (main group) of animals is divided. For example, the phylum chordata is divided into classes such as amphibians, reptiles, birds and mammals.

Cold-blooded Animals whose body temperature varies with their surroundings. The main group are warm-blooded animals.

Extinct When a particular species of living thing has died out and disappeared for ever.

Gills Body parts for breathing underwater. They are usually feathery or frilly and take in oxygen that has dissolved in the water.

Habitat Particular place with its own kinds of animals and plants, such as a pine wood, grassland, desert, seashore or deep seabed.

Herbivore An animal that eats mainly plant foods, such as leaves, fruits and seeds.

Hibernation When an animal's body temperature falls very low, usually to less than 10°C, and the animal falls into a deep sleep to survive the long, cold season.

Incisors Teeth at the front of the mouth, usually shaped like chisels with sharp straight edges for gnawing and nibbling.

Invertebrate An animal that does not have a backbone (vertebral column).

Keratin A tough substance that forms the horns, claws, hooves and nails of mammals, the feathers, beaks, claws and scales of birds, and the claws and scales of reptiles.

Kingdoms The largest groups into which living things are divided. Animals form the largest of these.

Larva The growing stage of a creature, such as an insect that looks different to its parent, for example, the caterpillar of a butterfly.

Mammary glands Parts on a female mammal's front that make milk for her young.

Marsupial A mammal whose young are born very tiny and undeveloped, and which continue to grow and develop in a pocket-like pouch on the front of the female's body.

Metamorphosis When an animal changes its body shape greatly as it grows, instead of the same body shape just growing larger.

Nymph The growing stage of an animal, such as an insect, which resembles its parent in general shape.

Ommatidia Tiny rod-shaped parts that together form the eye of an insect.

Omnivore An animal that eats a wide range of foods, both meat and plant matter.

Parasite A parasitic animal gains nourishment or shelter from another living thing, called its host, and in doing so, can damage or harm the host.

Phylum The main groups into which the animal kingdom is divided, such as sponges molluscs, echinoderms and annelid worms. Each phylum is divided into various classes.

Plankton Tiny plants and animals that drift in the water of seas, oceans and large lakes.

Predator An animal that hunts and catches other creatures, called prey, for its food.

Prey A creature that is hunted or caught as food by another animal, called the predator.

Pupa A hard-cased, inactive stage in the life of an insect before becoming an adult.

Scales Small, hard parts, usually in overlapping rows, covering the bodies of animals such as reptiles and fish.

Scavenger An animal, such as a vulture, that eats leftovers or the remains of dead animals' bodies.

Segments Ring-like parts of the body of an animal, such as a worm, which are all similar and joined together in a row.

Spawn A clump or cloud of eggs laid by a female animal, such as a frog or fish.

Species The groups into which animals are divided. All members of a species can breed together, but they cannot breed with members of other species.

Syrinx A body part similar to a voice-box, in the lower neck and upper chest of a bird. The syrinx makes loud sounds as the bird sings and calls.

Tentacle An arm- or leg-like body part that is very bendy all the way along, without special joints.

Thorax The name for the middle or chest region of the body in many kinds of animals. In an insect, the legs and wings join to the thorax.

Vertebrate An animal that has a backbone (vertebral column), usually as part of its inner skeleton of bones.

Warm-blooded When an animal's body temperature stays the same, despite changing temperatures in its surroundings. The two main groups of warm-blooded animals are mammals and birds.

Index

Entries in bold refer to main subjects; entries in italics refer to illustrations.

A
aardvark 14, *14*, 15
abdomen, insects 26, *26*
adders 21
albatross 16, 17
alligators 20
   American alligator 20, *20*
alpaca 13
amphibians 9, **22–23**
anaconda 21
anglerfish 25, *25*
anteater 14, 15
antelopes 12
antennae, insects 26
ants 28
apes 14, 15
aphids 29
arachnids 9, **30–31**
arapaima 24
arthropods 9, 26, 30
asses 12

B
Bactrian camel 13, *13*
barnacles 32
bats 11, *11*
beaks, birds 16, 18
bears 10, 11
beaver 12, *12*
bedbugs 29
bees 28, 29, *29*
beetles 9, 26, 28, 29
bills, birds 18
bird-eating spider 30, 31
birds 9, **16–19**
   beaks 18
   birds of prey 16, 17
   calls and songs 19
   colonies 19
   flightless birds 17
   nests 19
   nocturnal birds 17
   sea birds 17
bison 13, *13*
black bear 10
black caiman 20, *20*
black widow spider 31
blackbird 18
blackfly 29
blood-sucking insects 27
body temperature
   amphibians 22
   birds 16
   mammals 10

body temperature *(continued)*
   reptiles 20
bony fish 9
breathing
   amphibians 22
   crustaceans 32
   fish 24
   whales 10
breeding 9
brown bear 10
brown recluse spider 31
bugs 29
bushmaster 20
butterflies 28, *28*
butterfly fish 25
buzzards 16

C
caecilians 22, 23, *23*
caimans 20
calls, birds 19
camels 12, 13
camouflage 16
Carnivora 11
carnivores 11
carp 25
cartilage fish 9, 24
caterpillars 28, *28*
catfish 24
cats 9, 11, 14
cattle 12
cavies 12
centipedes 9, 30, *30*
cetaceans 11
chameleon 21
chordates 9
chrysalises, butterflies 28
cicadas 26, 29
civets 11
clams 34
claws, birds 16
cobras 21, *21*
cockles 35, *35*
coelacanths 25, *25*
cold-blooded animals 20, 22
colonies, birds 19
complete metamorphosis 28, *28*
condors 16
copepods 33, *33*
coral polyps 9, 35
coral reefs 25, 35
cowries 34
crabs 9, 32, 33, 35, *35*
crayfish 32
crickets 27
crocodiles 9, 20
   Nile crocodile 20, *20*

crocodilians 20, *20*
crossbill 18, *18*
crows 18
crustaceans 9, 30, **32–33**

D
daphnia 33
decapods 32
deer 9, 12
denticles, sharks' skin 24
desert tortoise 21, *21*
dinosaurs 8, 25
dogs 9, 11
dolphins 11, 32
dragonfish 25
dragonflies 26, 28
dromedary 13, *13*
dugongs 14

E
eagles 9, 16
earthworms 35, *35*
earwigs 28
Eastern newt 23, *23*
echidna 15
eels 24
eggs
   amphibians 22, 23
   birds 16, 19
   crocodiles 20
   crustaceans 32, 33
   egg-laying mammals 14, 15
   insects 28
   reptiles 20
   tortoises 21
   turtles 21
elephants 10, 13, *13*, 14
   African savannah elephant 13, *13*
emu 17
Eurasian kingfisher 18, *18*
Eurasian swift 19
eyes
   insects 27
   owls 17

F
falcons 16
false-scorpions 30
fanworms 35
feathers 16, 18, 19
fins, fish 24
fish 9, **24–25**
   deep-sea fish 25
   defences 25
   food 25
fish lice 33

flamingos 19, *19*
flatworms 9
fleas 27
flies 9, 27, 29
flippers 10, 11
flying foxes 11
food 8
   fish 25
   meat-eaters 11
   plant-eaters 12–13
foxes 9, 11
frilled lizard 21, *21*
frogs 9, 22, 23, *23*
fruit bats 11
fur 10

G
Galapagos iguana 21
gannets 16, 17, *17*
gazelles 12
geese 32
gharial 20, *20*
giant panda 10
giant salamander 22
giant squid 9, 11, *11*, 34
giant tortoise 21
gila monster 20
gills
   amphibians 22
   crustaceans 32
   fish 24
glands, mammary 10
gnats 26
goats 12
golden eagle 9, 16, *16*
goldfish 9
goliath spider 31
grasshoppers 27, 28
great green bush cricket 27, *27*
greenfly 29
grizzly bear 10
grubs 28
guanaco 13
guillemot 19
guinea pigs 12
gulls 19
gulper eel 25
gymnophions 23

H
habitats 8
hares 12
harriers 16
hawks 16, 17
hedgehogs 10, *10*
hellbender 22, *22*
herbivores 12–13

hermit crab 35
hibernation 10
hippo 12, 13
honeybees 29, *29*
hoofed mammals 12, 15
horses 12
housefly 9
human beings 10, 14
hummingbirds 18, *18*
hyaenas 11, *11*
hyraxes 13

I
iguana 21
incisor teeth, rodents 12
incomplete metamorphosis 28
insectivores 10
insects 9, **26–29**, 30
invertebrates 26
isopterans 27

J
jackals 11
jawless fish 9
jaws, snakes 21
jellyfish 9, 34, 35

K
kangaroos 9, 14, 15, *15*
katydids 27, *27*
kestrels 16
king cobra 21
kingfishers 18
kites 16
kiwi 17
komodo dragon 20
kookaburra 18
krill 11, 32, 33

L
lanternfish 25, *25*
larvae
   amphibians 22
   crustaceans 32
   insects 28
leeches 35
lice 33
limpets 34
linsangs 11
lionfish 25, *25*
lizards 9, 20, 21
llama 13
lobsters 32, 35, *35*
lungfish 24

M
mambas 21
mammals 9, **10–15**

mammals (*continued*)
   meat-eating 11
   plant-eating 12–13
   rare mammals 14–15
mammary glands 10
manatees 14, *14*
mantids 27
mantis shrimps 32, *32*
marsupials 14, 15
meat-eaters 11
metamorphosis
   amphibians 22, 23
   insects 28, *28*
Mexican beaded lizard 20
mice 12, 14
midget spider 30
migration, birds 19
milk, mammals 10
millipedes 9, 30, *30*
mites 30, *30*
mockingbird 19, *19*
moles 10, 14
molluscs 9, **34–35**, *35*
monitor lizard 21
monk seal 24, *24*
monkeys 9, 14, 15
monotremes 14
mosquitoes 27, *27*
moths 28
mussels 34–35, *35*

N
nests
   birds 16, 19, *19*
   termites 27
newts 22, 23
Nile crocodile 20, *20*
Nile monitor lizard 21
nocturnal birds 17
nymphs 28

O
oceans
   crustaceans 32–33
   fish **24–25**
   mammals 11
   seabirds 17
   turtles 21
octopuses 9, 34
opossums 14
ostrich 17, *17*
owls 9, 16, 17, *17*
oysters 34

P
panda 10
parasites 30, 33
parrot fish 25

parrots 18
peccaries 12
pelicans 16
penguins 16, 17, *17*, 32
periwinkles 35, *35*
phyla 9
pigs 12
pike 25
piranhas 25, *25*
plankton 24, 32
plant-eating mammals
   12–13
platypus 9, 15, *15*
plovers 19
poison-dart frog 22, *22*
poisons
   fish 25
   frogs and toads 22
   lizards 20
   millipedes 30
   molluscs 34, 35
   scorpions 31
   snakes 20, 21
   spiders 31
polar bear 10, *10*
pollination, flowers 29
pond-flea 33
pondskaters 29, *29*
porcelain crab 33, *33*
porcupines 12
porpoises 11
pouched mammals 15
prawns 32
praying mantis 27, *27*
primates 14, 15
puff adder 21, *21*
pupae, butterflies 28
pythons 21

R
rabbits 12
raccoons 11
ragworms 35
rails 17
raptors 16
rats 9, 12, 14
rays 9
razorshell 35, *35*
red fox 9, *9*
reptiles 9, **20–21**
rhea 17
rhino 12, 13
rodents 12

S
salamanders 9, 22, 23
salmon 9
saltwater crocodile 20

sand-hoppers 32
scales, fish 24
scorpions 9, 30, *30*, 31
sea anemones 9, 33, 34, 35,
   35
sea cows 14
sea cucumbers 34
sea lilies 34
sea-snakes 20
sea squirts 9
sea turtles 21, *21*
sea urchins 9, 34, 35, *35*
seabirds 17, 19
seals 10, 11, 14, 32
seas
   birds 17
   crustaceans 32–3
   fish 24–5
   mammals 11
   turtles 21
senses 8
sharks 9, 24
sheep 12
shellfish 34
shells
   crustaceans 32
   molluscs 34
   turtles and tortoises 21
shieldbugs 29
shrews 9, 10, 11, 14
shrimps 9, 32, *32*
sickle-billed vanga 18, *18*
sirenians 14
sirens 22, 23
skinks 21
slow-worms 21
slugs 34
snails 34
snakes 9, 20, 21
song thrush 19, *19*
songs, birds 19
sounds
   birds 19
   insects 26, 27
sowbugs 32
sparrows 9
species **8–9**, *9*
sperm whale 10, 11, *11*
spiders 9, **30–31**
spiny anteaters 15
spiny lobster 32, *32*
sponges 9, 34, 35, *35*
spoonworms 9
squat lobster 32
squid 9, 11, 34, *34*
squirrels 12
starfish 9, 34, *34*
stoats 11

stonefish 25, *25*
stonefly 28
storks 16, 19
swifts 19, *19*
syrinx 19

T
tadpoles 22, 23
talons, birds 16
tapirs 12
tarantulas 31, *31*
tawny owl 17
taxonomy 9
teeth
  aardvarks 15
  elephants 13
  rodents 12
  sharks 24
temperature, body
  amphibians 22

temperature, body
  (*continued*)
  birds 16
  mammals 10
  reptiles 20
tenrec 10
termites 27, *27*
thorax, insects 26, *26*
thread-snakes 21
thrushes 19
ticks 30, *30*
tiger shark 24, *24*
tigers 9
toads 22
torpor 22
tortoises 20, 21
treehoppers 29
tuatara 20
tubeworms 35
tubulidents 14

turtles 9, 20, 21
tusks, elephants 13

u
ungulates 12, 15

V
vertebrates 9
vicuna 13
viperfish 25
vipers 21
Virginia opossum 14, *14*
Vulpes vulpes 9
vultures 16

W
waders 19
wallabies 15
wandering albatross 16, 17
warm-blooded animals 10

wasps 27, 28
water beetles 29, *29*
water flea 32, 33, *33*
weasels 11
webs, spiders 30, 31, *31*
whales 9, 10, 11, 14, 32, 33
whelks 34, 35, *35*
white ants 27
wings
  bats 11
  beetles 29
  birds 16
  flightless birds 17, *17*
  insects 26, 27
woodlice 32
worm-lizards 20
worms 9, 35

Z
zebras 12, *12*

The publishers would like to thank the
following artists who have contributed to this book:
Lisa Alderson, Syd Brack, John Butler, Martin Camm, Jim Channell, Richard Draper, Wayne Ford,
Chris Forsey, Luigi Galante, Alan Harris, Ian Jackson, Mick Loates, Kevin Maddison, Alan Male, Maltings,
Janos Marffy, Andrea Morandi, Terry Riley, Steve Roberts, Eric Robson, Rudi Vizi

All other photographs are from:
Corel, DigitalSTOCK, digitalvision, MKP Archives, PhotoDisc